~ 1 ~

The facts of a February morning

The curtain rises
on a lone cabin in a clearing
big enough for corn.
Winter wind moans in the trees,
groans fitfully up the chimney
to seek the moon.
Soon, overhead, a rumpled hawk scans tracks
to the cabin's door—
help summoned
to labor's assizes.

BABY ABE

A Lullaby for Lincoln

by Ann Chandonnet

Illustrated by

Katie Scarlett Faile

This book is a publication of Circles, the children's book imprint
of Cirque Press, Anchorage, Alaska.

Library of Congress Cataloging-in-Publication Data

Chandonnet, Ann, 1943

Baby Abe: A Lullaby for Lincoln [Illustrated by] Katie Scarlett Faile
Summary: The first three years of Abraham Lincoln's life, 1809-1812, are presented
in free verse accentuated by a variety of rhyme forms and contemporary usages.
Provides a description of daily life in backwoods Kentucky and Indiana.

Includes: Author's Note, directions for creating A Pretzel Cabin [handicraft], instructions
for baking Mrs. Lincoln's Gingerbread Men [activity], Glossary and limited Chronology.

ISBN: 9798721903939 (softbound)
1. Lincoln, Abraham, 1809-1865. 2. Lincoln, Abraham, quotations.
3. Lincoln, Abraham, ancestors. 4. Lincoln, Abraham, childhood.
5. Lincoln, Abraham (AL's grandfather, killed 1786).
6. Thomas Lincoln (AL's father, died 1851).
7. Nancy Hanks Lincoln (AL's mother, died 1818).
8. Lincoln, Sarah (AL's older sister, "Sally," born 1807).

Graphic Design Dale Champlin

First Edition: July 2021
Printed in the United States of America

Circles
c/o Cirque Press
Sandra Kleven, Publisher
Michael Burwell, Editor
3157 Bettles Bay Loop
Anchorage, AK 99515
cirquepressaknw@gmail.com
907.764.1945

Dedications

Dedicated to my wonderful sons,
Alexandre (AKA "Baby Ah'wix"),
and Big Brother Yves who said "Hold 'em."

Additionally dedicated to my brother Duncan,
who can define "stone boat."

~Ann Chandonnet

For the bears, Erik and Brayden~
you are the peanut butter to my jam.

"Wherever the wind takes us. High, low.
Near, far. East, west. North, south~
we take to the breeze, we go as we please."
—*Charlotte's Web*

~Katie Scarlett Faile

Author's Note

This lullaby imagines scenes from Abraham Lincoln's life, from his 1809 winter arrival in the world to his third birthday (1812). Period objects, foods, verbal expressions and manners are twined into the text. Scenes described are typical of life on the Kaintuck (Kentucky) and Indiana frontiers. Research began with Carl Sandburg's two-volume biography; and, some years later, embraced the details of Sidney Blumenthal's *A Self-Made Man: The Political Life of Abraham Lincoln*, 1809-1849 (2016).

Characters are generally true to history with the exception of the preacher, the tinsmith, the shoemaker, the Yarb Woman and the Widder. Although fictional, these characters are typical of individuals who would regularly visit remote homesteads.

Cousin Dennis Hanks is one of the few family members whose pronouncements about the future of baby Abraham were recorded.

For readers who wish to know more about Abe from 7 to 21, see *Abe's Youth: Shaping the Future President.* Edited by William Bartelt and Joshua Claybourn. (Indiana University Press, 2019).

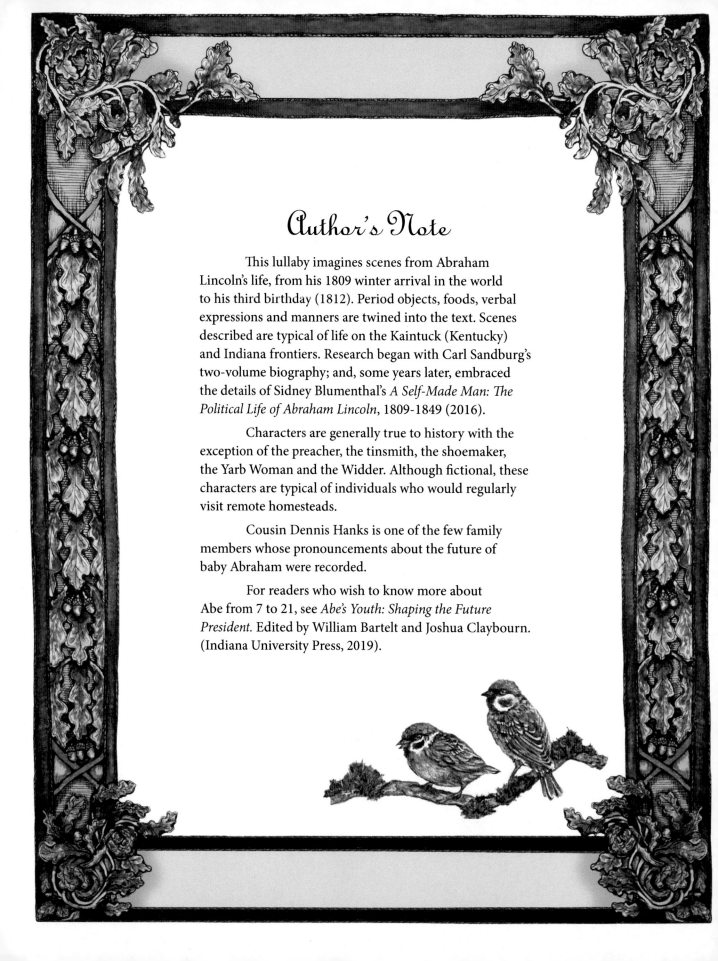

The tang of fresh nutmeg

rose to tickle Nancy Lincoln's nose.
Her weary eyes winked open.
She heard the clink of precious eggs plinked
on the edge of the old dry sink.
Her pinched mouth watered.

Storm harried the chinking.
Murmurs fell and rose,
rose and fell,
around Baby Abe.

Released from pain

Nancy Lincoln again licked her lips.
The Yarb Women were preparing a treat
to restore her hollowed body:
a warm, sweet nog.
(Nan had not tasted fresh nutmeg
since her wedding.)

Stretching her legs,
the new mother cautiously shifted her hips
beneath the cotton flannel sheet
and linsey-woolsey bedding~
down, down to find the balm
of the soapstone bed warmer.

Mid-day twilight
These were the sights

Straining, Nancy urged her chin past the bolster,
peered at the cradle beside the trundle.
There he nested:
a tight linen bundle—
Abraham, Baby Abe,
the boy Tom had prayed for.

Framed in a white cap,
Baby's lean, red face steamed
in the drafts swirling around the shutters.
(February was cold in Kaintuck.)

A panther's high-pitched, piercing scream
curled around the eaves like a goblin's charm
or a side-winding black snake.
Muttering sheaves of sleet pummeled the thin shakes.

Wolves outside sounded close

Inside, firelight cast
clogging clowns on the walls, the sanded floor.
Abe's eyes burst wide as doors,
glinting gems of curiosity and alarm.

Using a leg as a table,
Thomas Lincoln whittled a fierce sow
trailed by her cubs.
Then, reaching his rifle-gun down from its pegs
he walked out in search of game.

Icicles dripped

Tom Lincoln piggy-backed big sister Sarah
down from the warm loft
where she'd been chawing dried mint.
Sarah sank into the rocker, spread wide
her soft arms, said,
"Hold em! Hold em!"

Fearing harm

the Widder cautioned, "Tomorrow, Sarah.
Tomorrow. You'll have your stint.
Brother needs to be fed."
(She turned to slice bread.)
Pouting Sarah stuck out her lower lip.
She wanted to cuddle him now~

Baby Abe

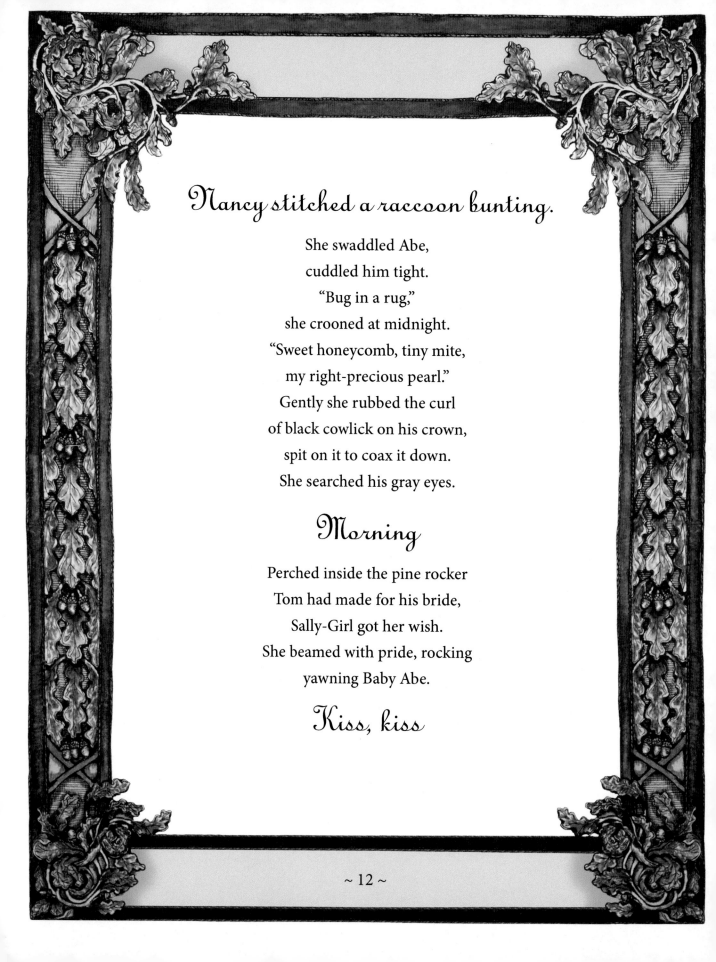

Nancy stitched a raccoon bunting.

She swaddled Abe,
cuddled him tight.
"Bug in a rug,"
she crooned at midnight.
"Sweet honeycomb, tiny mite,
my right-precious pearl."
Gently she rubbed the curl
of black cowlick on his crown,
spit on it to coax it down.
She searched his gray eyes.

Morning

Perched inside the pine rocker
Tom had made for his bride,
Sally-Girl got her wish.
She beamed with pride, rocking
yawning Baby Abe.

Kiss, kiss

Sleet withdrew
sky cleared

Bright stars winked so close, so close—
like a blessing on this fragile tyke.

This boy had big hands, big feet,
pitcher-handle ears:
He was not a pretty young'un.
Proud Thomas chopped wood in the lean-to,
then entered smelling of evergreen sap,
his cap and fur coat dusted with chips.
Loud Abe cried and cried.

"He'll never come to much,"
sighed Cousin Dennis Hanks
when he walked two miles to visit.

Sitting up now,
Nan thought otherwise~
swallowing her opinion to be polite.
"Prince of wails,"
"Butterfly boy," "Jam Roly Poly,"
Nan crooned to her sweeting.
(Did Dennis speak in spite?)

April offered dandelions spring tonic

Kettle steamed on the trivet.

Rye 'n Injun rose on the hearth.

On his stomach,

Little Abe strained to lift his heavy head.

Sooty kettle, sparks and ashes.

Dirt floor, corn-husk bed.

Nancy dared

to bathe Baby before the fire,

rubbed him with goose grease.

He stretched his knobby limbs.

"Spider child!"

marveled Nancy, re-wrapping his sinewy length.

"My fine foal, my wild colt."

She shed a few tears at his body's perfection,

at her endless love for him.

"I trap my rabbit by the ears!

I holt you by the nose!" she crowed.

He ceased yawning.

Baby Abe

Summer crept into the clearing.

The endearing babe grew like a thistle.
"My new broom," Nan chortled.
"You will sweep despair from your mother's eye."
(She surprised herself at what she said
of her Baby Abe.)

When she hung out the wash, she whistled.
Abe sat close.
He waved and kicked—sometimes sneezed,
sometimes bubbled a proclamation.
Squirrels approached to tease.

The wet heat of summer bears down.

Corn stalks flourish tassels
like bustles.

Under an oak in a willow basket,
Baby dozed on an old plaid shirt
while Nan weeded dill, sage, comfrey.
Red squirrel lobbed a green acorn.
Dark eyes fluttered wide.
Squirrel froze,
then flourished his tail to scold.

"Kitty," Abe hummed to the flirt in the trees.
"Kitty, come."

Nettle pollen, red dust plus
stream-side mold had him rubbing his nose,
stretching his toes.

Sweet Abe

One misty September morn

Nancy set her thriving pet on a torn sheet
in the swept front yard.
He could just manage sitting,
a crust of corn cake in each fist.
He'd tilt and sway a bit—
and track his shadow.

Leaves fell.
He slowly crept to them,
caressed, kissed, tasted—
decoded their rustles of conversation.

Sweet Baby Abe

Winter hushed forest noises

except for whistle of wind in mist.
Inside voices were:
burble of Hasty Pudding on the hob,
shuffling ox in the lean-to.
These whispers brought Abe to attention.
His face was kissed with wonder as he soaked up life
as yellow rice soaks up clabber.

Our housewife unpinned her silky hair,
swept it like a hank of yarn
over little Abe's sprouting nob
and bare torso.
He giggled and stared,
stared and giggled.
Jabbered.

O, O, Baby

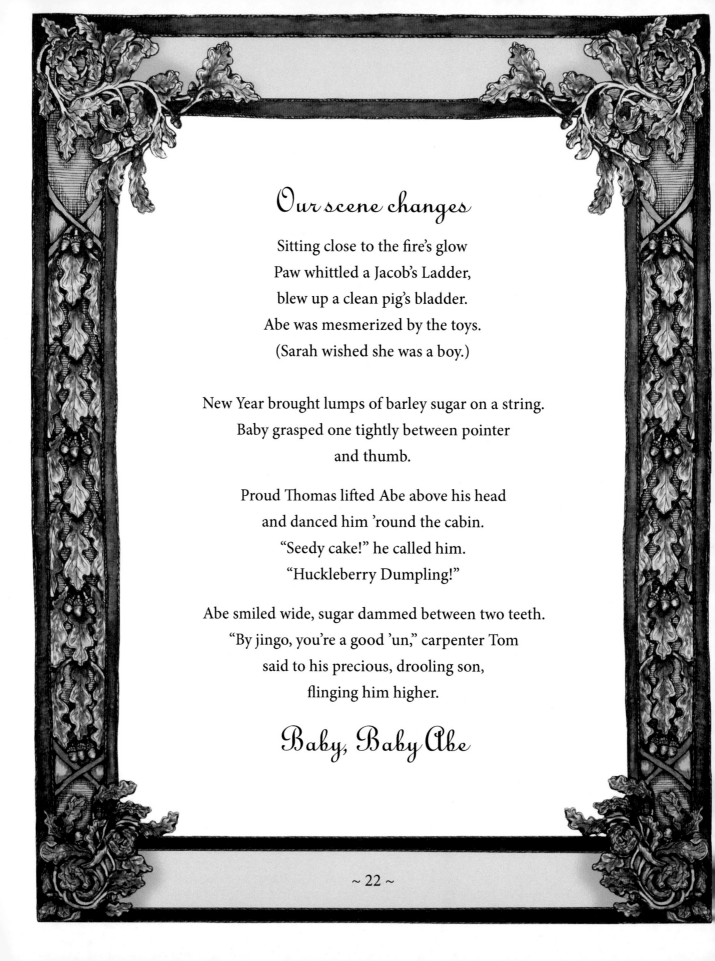

Our scene changes

Sitting close to the fire's glow
Paw whittled a Jacob's Ladder,
blew up a clean pig's bladder.
Abe was mesmerized by the toys.
(Sarah wished she was a boy.)

New Year brought lumps of barley sugar on a string.
Baby grasped one tightly between pointer
and thumb.

Proud Thomas lifted Abe above his head
and danced him 'round the cabin.
"Seedy cake!" he called him.
"Huckleberry Dumpling!"

Abe smiled wide, sugar dammed between two teeth.
"By jingo, you're a good 'un," carpenter Tom
said to his precious, drooling son,
flinging him higher.

Baby, Baby Abe

Watching a pan of gingerbread

preparing crust for pies,
busy Nancy beamed with pride.
Weary, weary, she sighed.

Baby Abe

One year old, hungry, hungry

At noon, Nancy basted a fat goose,
then blew on pease porridge in a wooden spoon,
set it on his nether lip and tongue.
His wizard eyes flew open.
at the strange green taste
of the hot green paste.

"Sweet one," Nancy crooned

"My shining one."
Baby Abe,
her precious son.

Baby Abe
gummed a stewed gizzard

Abe's second March

Eaves dripped sludge.
Abe scooted to the door propped ajar,
swatted at the bearskin hanging there.
He pinched its softness cautiously,
examined it closely, solemnly~like a judge.

Nancy deemed Baby capable of big things.

He was a silent, brooding mite, but she heard
within her son's quiet murmurs
a millstone's roar.
Worlds spun behind his gaze.

White ox staked out to graze,
Tom Lincoln sharpened his axe, then his hoe;
cleaned his rifle-gun.

Tom took a carpentering job

miles away at a new store.
At home, he repaired the wagon.
No time to hew puncheons
for the cabin floor.

When Tom was away,
stray fox
crossing the yard
was Nan's clock.

As April daylight died

Nan, sitting, leaned toward the birch embers
breathing in and out on the hearth,
in and out like the side of a sleeping beast—
or the hide on a crock of sourdough yeast.
(Sara and the babe slumbered.)

Heart still doubtful,
Nan stopped biting her thumb,
bent close to her knitting;
a gray wool sock for Thomas
was just turning its corner.

Baby Abe

When Tom hired out elsewhere,

Nan flinched
at every snapping twig,
every rustling shrub.

Wringing out spare shirts,
rubbing her lye-reddened wrists over the tub,
she was a stoat, a calf—
wolf pendant at her throat.

Now and again
in rare idle moments

Nan was struck with disturbing dreams.
It seemed that in Abe's age-old stare
roiled blue smoke, gray smoke,
dying cook fires;
ranks of spare men
stumbling forward in mired cloaks.
Nan imagined
distant gunshots and muffled cries.

To dismiss such trying thoughts,
she shook her head, hard.
Still her brow twisted in knots.

Abe was a tall toddler in short skirts.
She was proud of him;
bestowed kisses in pairs
with a fierce pride.
What could these images mean?

Yes, siree

Summer plowed on.
Vegetables to weed.
Corn to hoe.

As sweet Abe napped in the shade,
a wordless hymn of shuffling feet
and clanging chains
passed by on the Turnpike
(the old Cumberland):
a coffle,
a coffle,
hidden by trees and dense willows.
Ding, ring, ring.

Ring, ding, ding

Frail, haggard wraiths

clocked a fast pace
over root and rock.

Ring, ring, a ~ ding

Now you see
the chained ones stagger and fall at the brink,
collapse on scabbed knees,
creep to drink at the spring.

Cling, clink, ding

With surprise, tears came,
Nan dabbed her eyes.
Fear rose in her breast.
She dropped two wet socks.
Concerned, she sprang to her babe,
snatched up her prize.

Ring a ~ ding

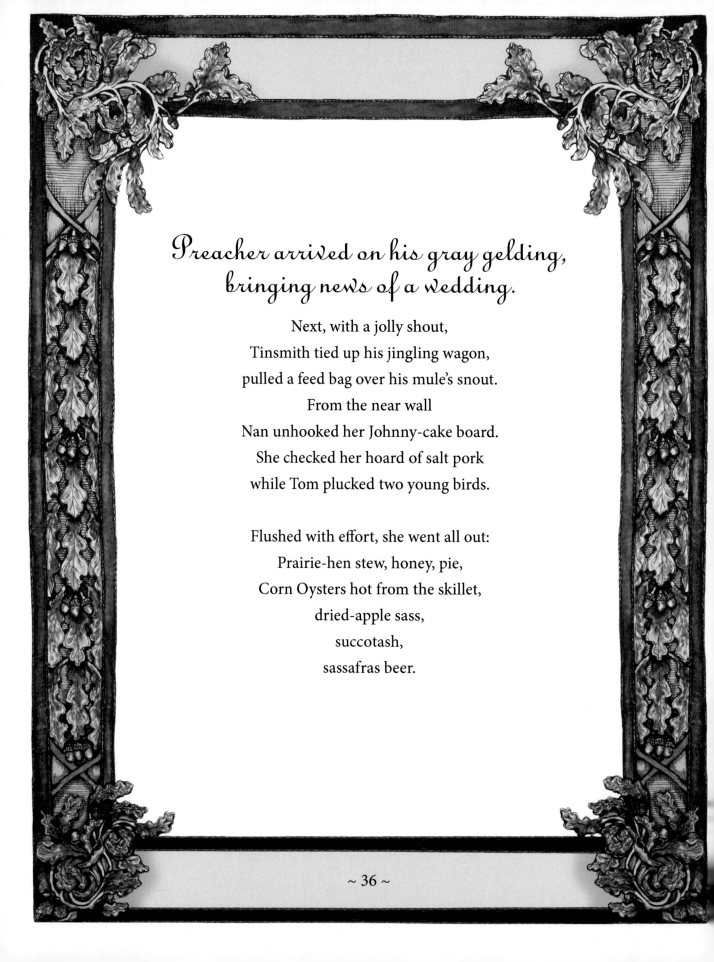

Preacher arrived on his gray gelding,
bringing news of a wedding.

Next, with a jolly shout,
Tinsmith tied up his jingling wagon,
pulled a feed bag over his mule's snout.
From the near wall
Nan unhooked her Johnny-cake board.
She checked her hoard of salt pork
while Tom plucked two young birds.

Flushed with effort, she went all out:
Prairie-hen stew, honey, pie,
Corn Oysters hot from the skillet,
dried-apple sass,
succotash,
sassafras beer.

Third visitor, young Shoemaker

He gladly shared news and gossip,
capered a jig,
tuned his fiddle,
posed new riddles.
Thomas needed shoes.

After two porringers of rabbit stew,
sly, red-headed Shoemaker urged Abe to reach
into the bumpy pocket of his smock.

Tentative, shy,
Abe withdrew a queer lump
that Shoemaker called
"a black rock that burns."
Both Nan and Abe were skeptical.
Abe tasted, shook his head—
tried to give it back.
(It was neither plum nor peach.)

Stalking fine ashes

Nan banished them—
first with her broom-corn broom,
last with a turkey wing fan.
She handed Abe a sturdy twig.
Sprawled on the cool dirt,
he learned fast,
all the while singing to himself,
"Can. Can. Can."
AAA
BB he scrawled.

𝒶

Abe fancied escape

He'd crab-scuttle across the floor
and out the door.
She flew to catch him.

Nancy handed Abe a rye biscuit
just to see him smile.
He could eat—and soon eat more.
In the rocker, she cuddled Abe a while,
Singing, "Ring-a-round the rosies,
Pocket full of posies."
Baby showed new teeth, bounced to the tune.

Spring returned with the robins.

Grouse drummed on the hill.
At the edges of the pasture
under a blooming cottonwood,
wild persimmon petals fell~
Snowflakes that could not melt.

Tom grew anxious, primed his rifle-gun
for big cats and hostiles.
Melted lead, molded it.

Sister Sarah's Sunday gown needed letting down.
She wheedled for a new one.
Like the proverbial stalk of weed,
her brother was sprouting out of his smock
once more.
Nancy kneaded Rye 'n Injun,
then handed Sarah her hemming work,
threaded two needles.

Her little boy,

Baby Abe

Summer stalked in
with battalions of deer ticks.

When Dennis walked again to visit,
fired up his corn cob pipe,
Abe could say his cousin's name.
Still, Dennis hugged his low opinion
of the solemn tad.

But now the able lad could gather kindling,
tie a square knot, even sup
rabbit broth from his tin cup.

Strong and placid, he rarely fussed.
But bad dreams haunted his sleep,
made him weep.

O, Baby Abe

The two children were sleeping.

Parents shared quiet talk before the dying fire.
"Mr. Lincoln," "Thomas" ~ just plain "Tom" now ~
dreamed of going out to Indiana.
His adventurous spirit was sold
on the notion of moving West.

"No doubt a'tall.
We otta go," he told Nan.
"Good land for grain ~ the best.
Tall timber, too," he'd been told.
"Good grazin'. We could get us a milch cow,
eat curds and whey."
Plans surged in his brain pan.
"Think on it a while."

Tom urged his wife toward a decision.
Nan bent her head over her mending
and swallowed bile.
"We'd need a little cash money," Tom schemed.
"No weeping, no weeping,"
Nan cautioned herself.

Foggy, foggy morn

Paw gone again,
Nan heard
a crowd approaching—
loud as hard-cider toasting on Muster Day.
(She even believed she smelled an ox roasting.)

A gay church supper?
A giddy election?
Abe's head, too, tilted in that direction.
And then Nan saw the V of geese emerge
above the corn.

The Lincolns moved ten miles to Knob Creek Farm.

Crops sown, hay mown, new fence built.

Abe soon repeated: "Knob Creek Farm."

He had just turned three.

It didn't seem possible.

Nan's Peaches 'n Honey,

her precious Apple Pan Dowdy.

Gray eyes, coal locks,

cheekbones sharp as a goose's breast bone.

skin like peach blow.

Not a sunny lad, but one who'd

be thrilled to his soul

to follow a hare or lynx to its lair,

trail the slow tread of a turtle.

He caught Monarchs, then let them go.

Gentle, curious Abe,

Abe of Knob Creek,

Abe of no clocks,

Abe of no socks

Chopping fodder or weeding

using a smudge in a knot to discourage flies,
he'd grab hold of a sliver like "prairie"
or "Hodgenville" and nudge it over his lips
all the live-long day ~
a bee quivering over a page of scarlet flowers
glimpsed in a borrowed book.

"Indiana, Indiana, Indiana ~"
the syllables
seemed to him like wagon wheels rolling
in narrow, dusty ruts,
or paddles stroking a wide river,
dugouts beached above a crooked falls.

Stew simmered
on a trammel hook.

Nan brewed rose hip tea,
sipped it from her one china cup.

He was doing so well~

Baby Abe
our Abe
Abraham Lincoln

END NOTES

Two Recipes

A Pretzel Cabin

When Abe's birthday rolls around, or snow creeps up to the windowpanes, celebrate by making a small log cabin.

Materials:
  ½ pint empty milk carton or larger
  Graham crackers
  Pretzel rods or thin pretzels
  textured crackers such as Wheat Thins
  creamy peanut butter or clear glue
  optional: brown paper bag or Kraft paper
  optional: candies that look like pebbles

Notes:

For the ½ pint carton, use small, straight pretzels. For a larger carton, use fatter pretzels—the ones called "rods."

Rinse carton with warm, soapy water and let dry overnight. Spread sides and top with peanut butter to cover surfaces. On one side, stick a two-part Graham cracker vertically as the door. On another side, stick a single square Graham as a window. Cut and arrange pretzel "logs" to cover all four sides. Even out the slope of the "roof" with peanut butter. Arrange crackers slightly overlapping, like "shingles."

This exercise is for young children who like to dip clean hands into gooey stuff. It can be a combination craft and snack event.

Older children can make a more permanent cabin by first covering the carton with Kraft paper, and allowing it to dry before pretzels are added. Clear glue is a neater alternative to peanut butter. Each wall or roof section must be allowed to dry (about an hour) before beginning on another. Royal Icing (that is, icing with egg whites) is another possibility.

Both chocolate malted milk balls and jelly beans are available in the form of realistic beach pebbles. Leave room on one side of the cabin to create a flat, one-layer chimney, narrowing at the top. Run beads of clear glue between the pebbles to secure them firmly. Allow to dry. Then add the small sections of log at each side of the chimney.

This method may also be used to make a three-sided shelter like the one the Lincolns lived from 1816 – 1817 at Little Pigeon Creek, Indiana.

Gingerbread Men

Nancy Lincoln did not own cookie cutters. (If she wanted a particular shape, she would cut it out freehand from stiff paper.) In Abe's day, any form of gingerbread—from cutouts of Minute Men to sticky slabs for lunch pails to moist cake—were all simply "gingerbread." This is how Abe refers to it during a debate with Stephen Douglas.

Nancy might have stretched her costly white flour with whole wheat flour, rye flour, stewed pumpkin or sweet potato. So the following instructions are a guide rather than an absolute rule.

Choose a basic gingerbread cookie recipe which includes molasses. Substitute sorghum for all or half the molasses. Use 1 tablespoon ground ginger to every 4 cups flour. Add cinnamon, cardamom and or freshly grated nutmeg to taste. Substitute lard for butter, margarine or oil. Make a fairly stiff dough, about the consistency of Silly Putty ®. Cover. Refrigerate overnight.

With greased hands, make golf-ball pieces. As if making a "snake," roll out balls one at a time on a lightly floured surface to make 12-inch long rods. Divide rods into two pieces. Fold the 9-inch length back on itself to form a "clothespin." This becomes the head, body and legs. Pinch to form "neck." The remaining 3-inch piece is laid across over the "neck" to make arms and hands. Use a fingertip to indicate feet and hands.

Nan did not have an oven. She made do with an open hearth. She would have baked gingerbread men on the floor of a cast iron skillet or kettle—a maneuver which took careful watching so as not to burn the cookies. Dutch settlers in New Amsterdam often had brick ovens built into their large fireplaces. This made it easier to bake bread and cookies. Note that the word cookie is derived from the Dutch *koekje*.

GLOSSARY

Apple Pan Dowdy An alternative to pie—and easier; peeled, sliced, sugared apples topped with biscuit dough and baked. On the frontier, apple slices were dried on string and kept for winter. To make a pie or dowdy, the slices would first be soaked overnight in water.

Bed Warmer Hard-back-book-size slabs of soapstone or other stone that resists cracking when heated. Warmers were heated in the fireplace before bedtime. Each slab had its own flannel cover, with a drawstring at one end.

Britches Beans Beans threaded on twine, dried in the pod; each pod resembles a pant leg.

Broom-corn A cultivated variety of sorghum, the panicles (tufts, flower clusters) of which are used to make brooms.

Chaw An old form of "chew," the verb as well as the substance (often tobacco) being chewed—but not swallowed.

Clabber Thickly curdled sour milk; bonnyclabber. A predecessor of yogurt.

Coffle A group of slaves chained together, driven along in a line down a narrow path or street.

Corn Oysters A cross between a Hush Puppy and Johnny Cake. These tasty fritters were enriched with whole corn kernels and whatever the housewife had available: eggs, milk, chicken fat, bacon drippings.

Divined Guessed.

Dry sink A piece of American furniture common before indoor plumbing. Essentially a plain wooden cabinet not unlike a dresser, but with two doors on the bottom, opening to shelves. Half of the top is lower than the other; a water pitcher and basin rested here, at a height convenient to a standing housewife/face splasher.

Flax An erect plant or shrub with blue flowers. The thread-like fibers of its stalk can be processed into linen threat. Nancy Lincoln was known as an excellent seamstress and a speedy flax spinner.

Flip A mixed drink of alcohol, sweetened and spiced.

Hanks, Dennis, friend (1799-1892), Nancy's cousin. After Abe's mother died of "milk sickness," Dennis moved into the loft of the Lincolns' cabin.

Hodgenville The name of the Kentucky town in the area where Lincoln was born.

Jacob's Ladder A popular folk toy deriving from "Genesis." As Jacob flees his murderous twin Esau, he dreams of a stairway to heaven, with angels ascending and descending. This amusing toy is composed of wooden blocks—each usually painted/dyed a different color. The flat blocks are held together by woven tape or string. When operated, the blocks give the illusion of cascading down the strings. Jacob's Ladder was one of the few amusements that children in Puritan American were allowed on Sundays.

In'jun old form of "Indian." "Native American" is now the proper term.

Johnny Cake or Journey Cake A tough, portable form of cornbread. "Johnnycake board" is a term for what modern cooks call a "pastry board."

Kaintuck, Kentucky The term "Kaintuck" was used to describe the state as well as rowdy boatmen who floated merchandise (including wheat and coal) down the Ohio and Mississippi from areas embracing the Ohio River Valley. More than 10,000 Kaintucks walked home from delivering goods to Nashville, TN, in 1810 alone. The 500-mile journey, on foot, took about 35 days. (The same method was used to transport naturally Y-shaped timbers ("knees") down the Merrimack to Boston's shipyard.) The roots of the term are unclear, but it seems to derive from an Iroquoian term meaning "(on) the meadow or "(on) the prairie." Another notion is that it is a Shawnee word, Kanta Aki, meaning "the Land of Those Who Became Our Fathers." It might also be related to the Mohawk *kenhta-ke*.

Lincoln, Sarah Bush Johnston, Lincoln's stepmother. An old friend of Thomas, now widowed, Sara marries Thomas Lincoln in 1819 and takes a neglected Abe in hand.

Link A torch. Translucent animal horn was also used as a container for carrying a light or ember.

Linsey-Woolsey A coarse twill or plain-woven fabric with a linen warp and a woolen weft. The word dates back to the 1400s. Warm and cheap and often woven at home, it was used for bed coverings, winter trousers and slave clothing.

Loose shakes Hand-made one by one, nails were rare and expensive on the American frontier. Roof shakes were often held down by sturdy branches reaching from side to side.

Lye A strong, caustic, alkaline substance created from wood ashes; mixed with bovine fat to make soap.

Milk sickness A fatal illness caused by drinking milk or eating meat from a cow that had grazed on poisonous plants. This was the cause of Nancy Lincoln's death.

Mid-wife, Yarb [Herb] Woman Tradition says a 14-year-old neighbor was sent to fetch midwives for Nancy Lincoln's lying in with Abraham. In the absence of a licensed physician, women living in remote places called upon experienced female neighbors to nurse them. Many older women possessed knowledge of botanical remedies.

Botanicals (folk medicines) were commonly used by Healers and Yarb Women. For example, corn silk was believed to encourage contractions of the uterus.

Nog Short for "eggnog," a nourishing combination of eggs beaten with milk or cream and sugar, commonly spiked with hard liquor. A little piece of wood. Also related to noggin, a wooden cup or mug suitable for serving a small quantity of ale; and a strong ale made in Britain. Heated with a poker, a nog was welcome before central heating, at taverns and during a medical emergency.

Nutmeg In Lincoln's day, nutmegs were sold whole. They needed grating before use in baking, punch, hot toddies and nogs.

Pease Dialect form of the plural of pea.

Puncheon A large, peeled log sawed in half lengthwise, so one side is flat. To make a rude cabin floor, the flat surfaces of logs are put top-most across a room, wall to wall. Round sides go down.

Pumpkin/pun'kin Dried pumping was as common a frontier ingredient as dried apples. Pumpkin or squash, rich in Vitamin A, helps heal the surfaces of the body, inside and outside, and makes hair shiny. Slices or circles of pumpkin were dried for winter meals, then hung on the walls near the fireplace or stored in the loft. Cooked, sieved pumpkin was often kneaded into bread dough.

Rick A stack of firewood in which each new layer is placed at a right angle to the previous one. Air flows freely, helping green wood dry.

Rye 'n Injun A dense, sustaining Colonial bread. A combination of half rye flour and half corn meal—cheaper than a loaf made solely from wheat flour. "Injun" is an old term for cornmeal, which Native Americans had introduced to early settlers. It is easier to grow rye than wheat.

Shoemaker's Last A wooden or cast iron form shaped like a human foot, used in the repair and manufacture of shoes. An itinerant shoemaker would carry several different sizes. When the last was in use, it was turned sole up and securely mounted to the top of a metal stand, to arrive at a comfortable working height. The shoe was assembled upon the last—which served as an inner pattern.

Short skirts Both boys and girls wore simple dresses for their first two years or so.

Sock, corner The most difficult part is turning the heel so the sole and ankle are at right angles.

Succotash A dish of corn kernels and shell beans simmered together. From Narragansett msickquatash. Colonists added milk and butter; Native Americans added raccoon fat or fish.

Sweeting A variety of apple; also, a cherished person. Term first used in the 13th century.

Widder A country form of "widow."

A BRIEF CHRONOLOGY

OF ABRAHAM LINCOLN

1637 Seventeen years after the Pilgrims settled in the New World, patriarch Samuel Lincoln or Linkhorn, a weaver's apprentice from Hingham, England, settled in Hingham, Massachusetts.

1778 Thomas Lincoln (Abe's father) is born in Virginia.

1780* After trekking over the Cumberland Gap, following early settlers like Daniel Boone, young Abraham Lincoln claims 3200 acres.

1786 Capt. Abraham Lincoln is ambushed and killed by Indians. His son, Thomas, 8 years old, escapes capture with the aid of an older brother.

1786-1806 Abandoned by his widowed stepmother, Thomas apprentices in Joseph Hanks' carpenter shop. He is also instructed by his Uncle Isaac's slaves on Isaac's Tennessee plantation. He becomes a "wandering labor boy" offering the combined skills of carpenter, mechanic and farmer.

1788 In Elizabethtown building a mill, Thomas hears an Emancipationist speak at the local Baptist Church.

1806 After a long acquaintance, Thomas Lincoln weds Nancy Hanks at the Harrodsburg Stockade.

1807 The Lincoln's first child, Sarah—nicknamed Sally—is born.

1808 Thomas Lincoln and his wife Nancy Hanks move, following antislavery pastor William Downs to settle in an existing cabin at Knob Creek Farm, near the Old Cumberland Trail.

Feb. 12, 1809 Birth of son to Thomas and wife Nancy at Sinking Spring Farm, by the south fork of Nolen Creek, in Hodgenville, KY. He is named Abraham.

Lincoln recalled those early days in verse:

When first my father settled here,
'Twas then the frontier line.
The panthers scream filled the night with fear
And bears preyed upon the swine.

December, 1816 When a suit is filed against his property, Thomas Lincoln crosses the Ohio River into Indiana, a new free state. The family hacks through dense wilderness to a building site. They subsist for two months in a half-tent or three-sided lean-to open to the weather, as Thomas erects a one-room cabin in the rural "community" of Little Pigeon Creek.

Abe is 7 years old. He later described this backwoods area: "We reached our new home about the time the State came into the union. It was a region with many bears and wild animals still in the woods. There I grew up."

October 5, 1818 Lincoln's mother, Nancy, dies. Thomas and Abe build her coffin. Later in life Abe declares fervently, "All that I am or ever hope to be, I owe to my angel mother. God bless her."

December 2, 1819 Thomas Lincoln marries Sarah Bush Johnston. A hard-headed widow, Sarah owns significant furniture, carried by wagon to her new home. She instructs her groom to floor and whitewash their residence.

1820 Sara insists that Tom send Abe to school. Young Abe loved learning. He borrowed books like *Aesop's Fables* and *Robinson Crusoe*. He would tuck a book in his shirt to read when taking a break from log splitting. Paper was scarce, so he wrote with charcoal on the back of a wooden shovel. He also wrote in dust and snow.

1820 At his mature height of 6'4" Abe at 11 was strong as an adult. But he yearned for a life of more than gritty labor. By existing tradition, Thomas owns Abe's labor until he reaches 21.

1821 Tom Lincoln builds the window frames, door casings and pulpit of Little Pigeon Creek Church.

1822*–1826* When not attending to chores at home or hired out by his father, Lincoln attends a "blab school"—no more than six months a year. A photo of this one-room rural Indiana school may be seen in *The Lincolns: A Scrapbook Look at Abraham and Mary*. A "blab" or "loud school" required students to recite at length as they mastered Read'n, Writ'n, and Cipher'n. Lincoln recited his lessons aloud during his walk home—a distance of more than four miles.

> He wrote in his arithmetic book:
> *Abraham Lincoln is my name*
> *And with my pen I wrote the same*
> *I wrote in both hast and speed*
> *And left it here for fools to read.*

Fall and winter 1826 –27 Abe works on a ferryboat on the Ohio River.

August 1826 Sarah Lincoln, Abe's sister, marries Aaron Grigsby, son of a well-to-do farmer.

January 20, 1828 Sarah Lincoln Grigsby dies in a complicated childbirth attended by a drunken physician. A weeping Abe, waiting in the smokehouse, hides his face in bony fingers and wails, "What do I have to live for?"

December 1828 Lanky Lincoln, 19, joins his cousin John Hanks in piloting a flatboat down the Mississippi. In New Orleans, what he sees of slave auctions angers him. His anger was so overwhelming, Hanks said, "We were afeared of getting into trouble about his talking so much, and we coaxed him with all our might to be quieter-like down there, for it wouldn't do no good no-how."

March 1830 Lincoln family moves from Indiana to homestead 162 acres on the Sangamon River in Illinois. Abe is now legally free of working solely for Thomas or for neighbors to whom his father hires him out. During their first summer here, Abe and Thomas hewed enough rails to fence 10 acres, and raised a corn crop.

1831 Despite his legal freedom, Abraham helps his father erect a cabin with two plank doors and glazed windows. A photo of this structure can be seen in Blumenthal's *A Self-Made Man: The Political Life of Abraham Lincoln*, 1809 –1849.

July 1831–April 1837 Lincoln settles in New Salem, a village near Springfield, IL. Boarding here and there while supporting himself with odd jobs, he educates himself in grammar, surveying and law. He reads extensively and listens to speeches during trials, at the Springfield Lyceum, around stoves in country stores, in smoky taverns, churches—almost anywhere.

August 6, 1831 Lincoln loses his first try at election for state senate.

1833 Cholera epidemic, Lexington.

September 9, 1836 Lincoln receives his license to practice law.

1838 First Lincoln-Douglas Debate, held in downtown Quincy, IL; 12,000 people from three states attend. (In the 1830s, Quincy was a major "station" on the Underground Railroad. Slaves would swim the Mighty Miss to make it to this safe harbor.)

1849 Cholera epidemic, Lexington.

Sept. 18, 1858 Twelve thousand people attend the fourth Lincoln-Douglas debate on the Coles County fairgrounds in Charleston. This site now houses the Lincoln-Douglas Debate Museum.

October 13, 1858 The sixth of the seven Lincoln-Douglas debates was again held in Quincy, a major port for riverboats on the Mississippi, located in Illinois where the Iowa and Missouri rivers meet. Lincoln expected to walk to the park where the debate was to be held in the open air, but the town had a sort of parade float, a boat on wheels for him to ride in. The boat was captained by a live raccoon.

February 11, 1861 Anticipating continuing civil unrest, Lincoln says goodbye to the citizens of Springfield, IL: "Let us confidently hope that all will yet be well."

*Dates unclear.

ALSO BY ANN CHANDONNET

At the Fruit-Tree's Mossy Root (1969, 1976, 1980, 1984)

The Complete Fruit Cookbook (1972)

The Cheese Guide & Cookbook (1973)

The Wife & Other Poems (1976)

The Wife: Part 2 (1979)

Ptarmigan Valley: Poems of Alaska (1980)

Auras, Tendrils: Poems of the North (1984)

Canoeing in the Rain: Poems for my Aleut-Athabascan Son (1990)

The Alaska Heritage Seafood Cookbook (1995, 2021)

Anchorage: Early Photos of the Great Land (2000)

Gold Rush Grub: From Turpentine Stew to Hoochinoo (2005)

Alaska's Inside Passage (Compass American Guides, 2006, second edition 2009)

"Write Quick": War and a Woman's Life in Letters, 1835-1867 (2010)

The Pioneer Village Cookbook: Reliable Receipts & Curious Remedies (2010)

Colonial Food (2013)

Barn Raisings and Cemetery Cleanings: An American Celebrations Cookbook (2016)

Author and Illustrator

Ann Chandonnet

Raised on a colonial land grant, author Ann Chandonnet swallowed a deep sense of history as present. A former college English instructor and police reporter, Chandonnet intends her lullaby to reinvigorate interest in Abraham Lincoln's formative years. Abe was a country boy, just three generations from the Linkhorns of Britain. How did an obscure frontier lawyer and government representative rise to become America's greatest leader?

Chandonnet has won a national prize for wilderness poetry as well as national and state awards for educational writing. She has been nominated three times for the Pushcart Prize. She is also the author of the "Alaska Food" article in the *Encyclopedia of American Food and Drink* (Oxford University Press).

Katie Scarlett Faile

The detailed watercolor originals in *Baby Abe* were created by Katie Scarlett Faile, a submariner's wife residing on the island of Guam. Faile's work has been influenced by greats including Carl Larson, Inge Look and Arthur Rackham. The decorative borders of *Baby Abe* combine the swirls and eddies of Van Gogh's "Starry Night" with the floral minutiae of William Morris.

Faile grew up in rural Georgia and took to visual art early. Her work has been widely featured in New England museums and magazines as well as naval ceremonies and submarine memorabilia. Her paintings and drawings have influenced the design of coins and also been used to adorn calendars, greeting cards and china.

ABOUT CIRCLES

Announcing Circles, a new imprint of Cirque Press designed for illustrated books.
Look to these engaging books for image and light, fun and fantasy, mystery and music.
Circles focuses on the singing of the spheres, the clock of the seasons, the mirth of the hyena,
and the renewal of legend and myth.

Sandra Kleven – Michael Burwell, publishers and editors

Circles
An Imprint Of Cirque Press

AUTHENTICITY

The "core authenticity"
of Colonial Williamsburg
was repeatedly consulted for details,
including clothing, food, tools, and
early quilt patterns.

Comments About *Baby Abe*

…Abe's love of language was central to his being—as his famous speeches attest, as well as the fondly recorded jokes and witticisms. He deeply understood, and felt, the power of words… I think he'd be pleased, even enchanted, by the characters in Chandonnet's "lullaby." This generative and generous book invites readers of any age or nation to ponder a time when people were every bit as deeply divided as we are now on this globe, but with no such poisonous meme as the notion of "alternative facts" to hobble us. *Baby Abe* is an American history source book perfectly suited to our times. It's also a paean to the importance of decency, dignity and truth for a nation and its leaders.

—Jean Anderson, fiction writer, critic, author of *In Extremis and Other Alaskan Stories* and *Human Being Songs: Northern Stories*

I find *Baby Abe* deep and sweet and full of social history. It is the sort of book that an adult can read and reread with a child over and over and still have more to learn from it. As the reviews may say, "destined to become a classic."

—Charlynn Lewis, retired third grade teacher; teacher of English as a second language, Saint Peters, MO

With precise, poetic language, Chandonnet evokes the early years of America's 16th President. Young readers interested in history will enjoy the glimpses of Abraham Lincoln as a baby, as well as the accompanying notes explaining historical and regional terms as well as culinary delights. The book encourages a vivid imagining of early childhood in Kentucky, presenting readers with the cultural and societal influences that shaped *Baby Abe*.

—Emily J. Madsen, Assistant Professor of English, University of Alaska Anchorage

If you love history you will enjoy Ann Chandonnet's lullaby about the first three years of our 16th President, Abraham Lincoln. Ann has the talent of showing history in a way that keeps the reader's attention to the end.

—Dianne A. Tobin, Clinical Family Nurse Practitioner

Ann Chandonnet has cleverly mixed a 'Lullaby for Lincoln' with the every day reality of Kentucky [1809 – 1812]—of the food, expressions, anticipations and moments of joy, sadness and forward looking. Some of the poems rhyme, others are blank verse but together they paint an era with words and expressions lost even to today's historians. The illustrations add to the narrative rather than just being "artwork to fill a blank part of a page."

—Steve Levi, historian, novelist, author of *Alaska Gold Rush, Boom or Bust in the Alaska Gold Fields* and *Cowboys of the Sky*

Made in the USA
Columbia, SC
24 August 2021